First Published in the UK in September 2013 by Focus Education (UK) Ltd
Updated December 2013

Focus Education (UK) Ltd
Talking Point Conference and Exhibition Centre
Huddersfield Road
Scouthead
Saddleworth
OL4 4AG
Focus Education (UK) Ltd - Reg. No 4507968

ISBN 978-1-909038-18-9

Companies, institutions and other organisations wishing to make bulk purchases of books published by Focus Education should contact their local bookstore or Focus Education direct:
Customer Services, Focus Education, Talking Point Conference and Exhibition Centre,
Huddersfield Road, Scouthead, OL4 4AG
Tel 01457 821818 Fax 01457 878205

www.focus-education.co.uk
customerservice@focus-education.co.uk
Printed in Great Britain by Focus Education UK Ltd.
Scouthead

Users should be fully aware that the DFE may change any element of their descriptors and guidance
This document was accurate at the date of publication.

Progression in the (new) National Curriculum

Introduction

The purpose of this document is to help teachers and school leaders quickly see progression in the National Curriculum (2014).

- The content for English and mathematics is outlined by strand. This enables a quick view of the end of year expectations. These charts are useful for teachers when planning for differentiation and challenge.

- The content for science is outlined by end of unit expectations on a year group basis.

- The content for the other subjects is outlined by end of key stage expectations.

Users should be fully aware that the Department for Education may change any element of these descriptors. This document was wholly accurate at the date of publication – in line with The National Curriculum in England: Framework Document (Dec 2013).

Contents

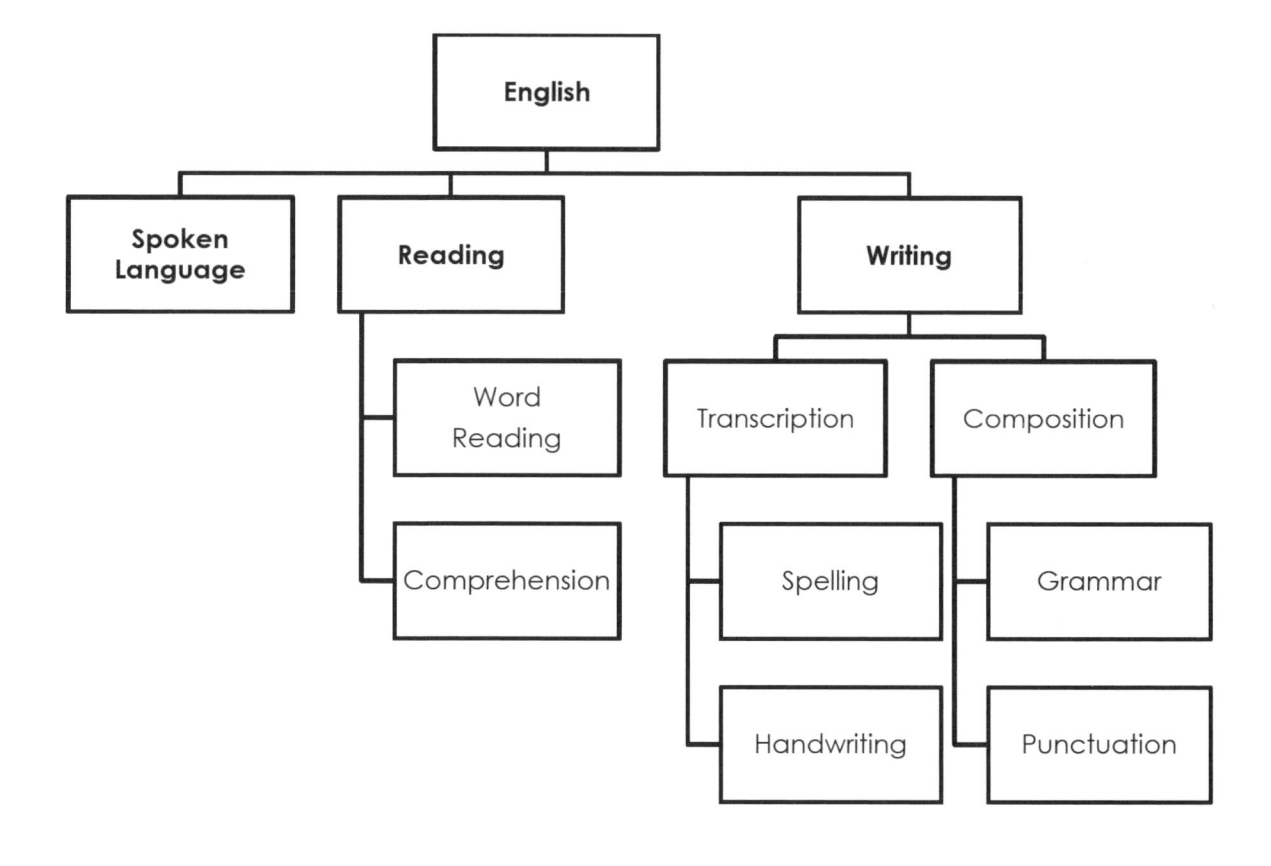

Spoken language

Years 1-6	Children should be taught to:

Children should be taught to:

- Listen and respond appropriately to adults and their peers

- Ask relevant questions to extend their understanding and build vocabulary and knowledge

- Use relevant strategies to build their vocabulary

- Articulate and justify answers, arguments and opinions

- Give well-structured descriptions, explanations and narratives for different purposes, including for expressing feelings

- Maintain attention and participate actively in collaborative conversations, staying on topic and initiating and responding to comments

- Use spoken language to develop understanding through speculating, hypothesising, imagining and exploring ideas

- Speak audibly and fluently with an increasing command of Standard English

- Participate in discussions, presentations, performances, role play, improvisations and debates

- Gain, maintain and monitor the interest of the listener(s)

- Consider and evaluate different viewpoints, attending to and building on the contributions of others

- Select and use appropriate registers for effective communication

Reading: Word reading							
Rec/ELG	Y1	Y2	Y3		Y4	Y5	Y6
	Apply **phonic knowledge** & skills as the route to decode words.	Continue to apply **phonic knowledge** & skills as the route to decode words until automatic decoding has become embedded & reading is fluent.					
	Respond speedily with the correct sound to **graphemes** for all 40+ phonemes, including, where applicable, alternative sounds for graphemes.	Read accurately by **blending** the sounds in words that contain the **graphemes** taught so far, especially recognising alternative sounds for graphemes.					
	Read accurately by **blending** sounds in unfamiliar words containing GPCs that have been taught.						
Use **phonic knowledge** to decode regular words and read them aloud accurately. ELG Read some **common irregular words**. ELG	Read **common exception words**, noting unusual correspondences between spelling and sound and where these occur in the word.	Read further **common exception words**, noting unusual correspondence between spelling & sound and where these occur in the word.	Read further **exception words**, noting the unusual correspondences between spelling and sound, and where these occur in the word.				
	Read words containing **taught GPCs** and –s, -es, -ing, -ed, -er and –est endings.						
	Read other **words of more than one syllable** that contain taught GPCs.	Read accurately **words of two or more syllables** that contain the taught GPCs.					
	Read words with **contractions**, e.g. *I'm, I'll, we'll* and understand that the apostrophe represents the omitted letter(s).						
		Read most words quickly and accurately, **without overt sounding & blending**, when they have been frequently encountered.					
	Read aloud accurately books that are consistent with their developing phonic knowledge and that do not require them to use other strategies to work out words.	**Read aloud** books closely matched to their improving phonic knowledge, sounding out unfamiliar words accurately, automatically & without undue hesitation.					
	Re-read these books to build up their **fluency & confidence** in word reading.	Re-read these books to build up their **fluency & confidence** in word reading.					
		Read words containing common **suffixes**.	Apply their growing knowledge of root words, **prefixes and suffixes** (etymology and morphology), both to read aloud and to understand the meaning of new words they meet.			Apply their growing knowledge of **root words, prefixes and suffixes** (etymology and morphology), both to read aloud and to understand the meaning of new words they meet.	

This page is intentionally blank

Reading: Comprehension[1]						
Rec/ELG	**Y1**	**Y2**	**Y3**	**Y4**	**Y5**	**Y6**
	Develop **pleasure** in reading, **motivation** to read, and **understanding** by:		Develop **positive attitudes** to reading and **understanding** of what they read by:		Maintain **positive attitudes** to reading and **understanding** of what they have read by:	
	Listening to & **discussing** a wide range of poems, stories & non-fiction at a level beyond that at which they can read independently	**Listening** to, **discussing** & expressing views about a wide range of contemporary & classic poetry, stories & non-fiction at a level beyond that at which they can read independently	**Listening** to and **discussing** a wide range of fiction, poetry, plays, non-fiction and reference books or textbooks		Continuing to **read** & **discuss** an increasingly wide range of fiction, poetry, plays, non-fiction and reference books or textbooks.	
	Being encouraged to **link what they read** or hear read to their own experiences					
		Discussing the **sequence of events** in books & how items of information are related.	Reading books that are **structured** in different ways and reading for a **range of purposes**.		Reading books that are **structured** in different ways and reading for a **range of purposes**.	
			Using **dictionaries** to check the meaning of words that they have read.			
	Becoming very **familiar** with key stories, fairy stories & traditional tales, retelling them & considering their particular characteristics	Becoming increasingly **familiar** with & retelling a wider range of stories, fairy stories & traditional tales.	Increasing their **familiarity** with a wide range of books, including fairy stories, myths, legends, and retelling of some of these orally.		Increasing their **familiarity** with a wide range of books, including myths, legends & traditional stories, modern fiction, fiction from our literary heritage, and books from other cultures and traditions.	
					Recommending books that they have read to their peers, giving reasons for their choices.	
	Recognising & joining in with **predictable phrases**	Recognising simple **recurring literary language** in stories & poems.				
		Discussing their favourite words & phrases.	Discussing words & phrases that **capture the reader's interest** and imagination.			
			Identifying **themes & conventions** in a wider range of books.		Identifying & discussing **themes & conventions** in and across a wide range of writing.	
					Making **comparisons** within & across books.	
			Recognising some **different forms of poetry** (e.g. free verse, narrative poetry).			
	Learning to appreciate **rhymes & poems**, and to recite some by heart	Continuing to build up a repertoire of **poems** learnt by heart, appreciating these & reciting some, with appropriate intonation to make the meaning clear.	Preparing **poems** and **play scripts** to read aloud and perform, showing understanding through intonation, tone, volume and action.		Learning a wider range of **poetry** by heart. Preparing **poems** and **plays** to read aloud and to perform, showing understanding through intonation, tone and volume so that the meaning is clear to an audience.	
		Being introduced to **non-fiction** books that are structured in different ways.				
	Discussing **word meanings**, linking new meanings to those already known.	Discussing & clarifying the **meaning of words**, linking new meanings to known vocabulary.				

Reading: Comprehension[2]

Rec/ELG	Y1	Y2	Y3	Y4	Y5	Y6
Read & **understand** simple sentences. ELG Demonstrate **understanding** when talking to others about what they have read. ELG	**Understand** both the **books they can already read accurately and fluently** and those they **listen to** by:		**Understand** what they read, in **books they can read independently**, by		**Understand** what they read by:	
	Drawing on **what they already know** or on background information & vocab provided by the teacher.	Drawing on **what they already know** or on background information & vocab provided by the teacher.				
	Checking that the text **makes sense** to them as they read & correcting inaccurate reading.	Checking that the text **makes sense** to them as they read & correcting inaccurate reading.	Checking that the text **makes sense** to them, discussing their understanding & explaining the meaning of the words in context.		Checking that the book **makes sense** to them, discussing their understanding & exploring the meaning of the words in context.	
	Discussing the significance of the title & events					
	Making **inferences** on the basis of what is being said & done	Making **inferences** on the basis of what is being said & done	Drawing **inferences** such as inferring characters' feelings, thoughts & motives from their actions, & justifying inferences with evidence		Drawing **inferences** such as inferring characters' feelings, thoughts & motives from their actions, and justifying inferences with evidence.	
	Predicting what might happen on the basis of what has been read so far	**Predicting** what might happen on the basis of what has been read so far	**Predicting** what might happen from details stated & implied		**Predicting** what might happen from details stated and implied.	
		Answering & asking **questions**	Asking **questions** to improve their understanding of the text.		Asking **questions** to improve their understanding.	
					Provide reasoned justifications for their views.	
					Discuss & evaluate how authors **use language**, including figurative language, considering the impact on the reader.	
			Identifying **main ideas** drawn from more than one paragraphs & summarise these.		Summarising the **main idea** drawn from more than one paragraph, identifying key details that support the main ideas.	
			Identifying how **language, structure & presentation** contribute to meaning.		Identifying how **language, structure & presentation** contribute to meaning.	
			Retrieve & record information from non-fiction..		Retrieve, record & present information from **non-fiction**.	
					Distinguish between statements of **fact & opinion**.	
	Participate in **discussion** about what is being read to them, taking turns & listening to what others say.	Participate in **discussion** about books, poems & other words that are read to them & those that they can read for themselves, taking turns & listening to what others say.	Participate in **discussion** about both books that are read to them and those that they can read for themselves, taking turns & listening to what others say.		Participate in **discussion** about both books that are read to them and those that they can read for themselves, building on their own & others' ideas & challenging views courteously.	
	Explain clearly their **understanding** of what is read to them.	Explain & discuss their **understanding** of books, poems & other material, both those that they listen to & those that they read for themselves.			Explain & discuss their **understanding** of what they have read, including through formal presentations and debates, maintaining a focus on the topic and using notes where necessary.	

READING

Writing: Handwriting						
Rec/ELG	Y1	Y2	Y3	Y4	Y5	Y6
	Sit correctly at table, holding pencil comfortably and correctly.					
	Begin to form **lower-case** letters in the correct direction, starting and finishing in the right place.	Form **lower-case** letters of the correct size relative to one another.				
		Start using some of the diagonal & horizontal strokes needed to **join letters** and understand which letters, when adjacent to one another, are best left unjoined.	Use the diagonal & horizontal strokes needed to **join letters** and understand which letters, when adjacent to one another, are best left unjoined.			
	Form **capital letters**.	Write **capitals** of the correct size, orientation and relationship to one another and to lower case letters.				
		Use **spacing** between words that reflects the size of the letters.				
	Form **digits** 0 – 9.	Write **digits** of the correct size and orientation.				
	Understand which letters belong to which handwriting 'families' and practise these.					
			Increase the **legibility**, **consistency** and **quality** of handwriting, e.g. by ensuring that down strokes of letters are parallel and equidistant; that lines of writing are spaced sufficiently so that the ascenders and descenders of letters do not touch.		Write **legibly**, **fluently**, with increasing **speed** by: - choosing which shape of letter to use when given choices and deciding whether or not to join specific letters - choosing the writing implement that is best suited for the task	

WRITING

Writing: punctuation & grammar

	Rec/ELG	Y1	Y2	Y3	Y4	Y5	Y6
Sentence structure	Write simple sentences which can be read by themselves and others. [Part of ELG]	How words can combine to make sentences. Joining words and joining sentences using and.	Subordination (using when, if, that, because) and co-ordination (using or, and, or but). Expanded noun phrases for description and specification (e.g. the blue butterfly). How the grammatical patterns in a sentence indicate its function as a statement, question, exclamation or command.	Expressing time, place and cause using conjunctions (e.g. when, so, before, after, while, because), adverbs (e.g. then, next, soon, therefore) or prepositions (e.g. before, after, during, in because)	Noun phrases expanded by the addition of modifying adjectives, nouns and preposition phrases (e.g. the teacher expanded to: the strict maths teacher with curly hair). Fronted adverbials (e.g. Later that day, I heard bad news).	Relative clauses beginning with who, which, where, why, whose, that o.an omitted relative pronoun. Indicating degrees of possibility using adverbs (e.g. perhaps, surely) or modal verbs (e.g. might, should, must).	Use of the passive voice to affect the presentation of information in a sentence. The difference between structures typical of informal speech and structures appropriate for formal speech and writing (such as the use of question tags, e.g. He's your friend, isn't he?, or the use of subjunctive forms such as If I were or Were they to come in some very formal writing and speech)
Text structure		Sequencing sentences to form short narratives.	Correct choice and consistent use of the present tense and past tense throughout writing. Use of the progressive form of verbs in the present and past tense to mark actions in progress.	Introduction to paragraphs as a way to group related material. Headings & sub-headings to aid presentation. Use of the present perfect form of verbs instead of the simple past (e.g. He has gone out to play contrasted with He went out to play)	Use paragraphs to organise ideas around a theme. Appropriate choice of pronoun and noun within and across sentences to aid cohesion and avoid repetition.	Devices to build cohesion within a paragraph (e.g. then, after that, this, firstly). Linking ideas across paragraphs using adverbials of time (e.g. later), place (e.g. nearby), number (e.g. secondly) and tense choice (e.g. he had seen her before).	Linking ideas across paragraphs using a wider range of cohesive devices: repetition of word or phrase, grammatical connections (e.g. the use of adverbials such as on the other hand, in contrast, or as a consequence) and ellipsis. Layout devices, such as headings, sub-headings, columns, bullets, tables, to structure text.
Punctuation		Separation of words with spaces. Introduction to capital letters, full stops, question marks & exclamation marks to demarcate sentences. Capital letters for names and the personal pronoun I.	Use of capital letters, full stops, question marks and exclamation marks to demarcate sentences. Commas to separate items in a list. Apostrophes to mark where letters are missing in spelling & to mark singular possession in nouns.	Introduction to inverted commas to punctuate direct speech.	Use of inverted commas and other punctuation to indicate direct speech. Apostrophes to mark plural possession. Use of commas after fronted adverbials.	Brackets, dashes or commas to indicate parenthesis. Use of commas to clarify meaning or avoid ambiguity.	Use of semi-colon, colon and dash to mark the boundary between independent clauses. Use of the colon to introduce a list and use of semi-colon within lists. Punctuation of bullet points to list information. How hyphens can be used to avoid ambiguity.
Terminology		letter, capital letter; word, singular, plural; sentence; punctuation, full stop, question mark; exclamation mark	noun, noun phrase; statement, question, exclamation, command; compound, suffix; adjective, adverb, verb; tense (past, present); apostrophe, comma	preposition, conjunction; word family, prefix; clause, subordinate clause; direct speech; consonant, consonant letter; vowel, vowel letter; inverted commas (or 'speech marks')	determiner; pronoun, possessive pronoun; adverbial	modal verb, relative pronoun; relative clause; parenthesis, bracket, dash; cohesion, ambiguity	subject, object; active, passive; synonym, antonym; ellipsis, hyphen, colon, semi-colon, bullet points

Writing: composition							
Rec/ELG	Y1	Y2	Y3	Y4	Y5	Y6
		Develop **positive attitudes** towards & **stamina** for writing by writing: - narratives about personal experiences and those of others (real and fictional) - about real events - poetry - for different purposes				
	Plan writing Say out loud what they are going to write about	**Plan writing** Plan or say out loud what they are going to write about Write idea and/or key words including new vocab.	**Plan writing** Discuss writing similar to that which they are planning to write in order to understand and learn from its structure, vocabulary and grammar. Discuss and record ideas.		**Plan writing** - Identify audience and purpose, selecting appropriate form and use other similar writing as model - Note and develop initial ideas, drawing on reading & research where necessary - In writing narratives, consider how authors have developed characters and settings in what pupils have read, listened to & seen performed	
	Drafting and writing Compose a sentence orally before writing.		**Drafting and writing** Compose & rehearse sentences orally (including dialogue), progressively building a varied & rich vocabulary & increasing range of sentence structures.		**Drafting and writing** Select appropriate grammar and vocab, **understanding how such choices can change and enhance meaning**	
	Sequence **sentences** to form short narratives.	Encapsulate what they want to say, **sentence by sentence**.	Organise **paragraphs** around a theme		Use a wide range of devices to build cohesion within and across **paragraphs**.	
					Précis longer paragraphs.	
Write **simple sentences** which can be read by themselves and others. [Part of ELG]			In **narratives**, create settings, characters & plot		In **narratives**, describe settings, characters and atmosphere and integrate dialogue to convey character and advance the action	
			In **non-narrative** material, use simple organisational devices such as headings and sub-headings		Use further organisational and presentational devices to structure text and guide the reader (e.g. headings, bullet points, underlining).	
		Make **additions, revision and corrections** to their own writing by: - Evaluating their writing with the teacher or other pupils - Re-reading to check it makes sense and that verbs to indicate time are used correctly & consistently, incl verbs in the continuous form	**Evaluate & edit:** - Assess the effectiveness of their own and others' writing and suggest improvements - Propose changes to grammar & vocab to improve consistency, including the accurate use of pronouns in sentences		**Evaluate & edit:** - Assess the effectiveness of their own and others' writing - Propose changes to grammar, vocab and punctuation to enhance effects and clarify meaning - Ensure the consistent and correct use of tense throughout a piece of writing - Ensure correct subject and verb agreement when using singular and plural, distinguishing between the language of speech and writing and choosing the appropriate register	
	Re-read what they have written to check that it makes sense	**Proof read** to check for errors in spelling, grammar and punctuation	**Proof read** for spelling and punctuation errors.		**Proof read** for spelling and punctuation errors.	
	Discuss what they have written with the teacher or other pupils. **Read aloud** their writing clearly enough to be heard by their peers and the teacher.	**Read aloud** their writing with appropriate intonation to make the meaning clear.	**Read aloud** their writing, to a group or whole class, using appropriate intonation and controlling the tone and volume so that the meaning is clear.		**Perform** their own compositions, using appropriate intonation, volume, and movement so that meaning is clear.	

WRITING

Writing: Spelling

Rec/ELG	Y1	Y2	Y3	Y4	Y5	Y6
	Spell words containing each of the 40+ **phonemes** already taught	Spell by segmenting words into **phonemes** and representing these by graphemes, spelling many correctly				
		Learn new ways of spelling **phonemes** for which one or more spellings are already known, & learn some words with each spelling, including a few common homophones.				
	Spell common **exception words**	Spell common **exception words**				
		Spell more words with **contracted** forms				
Use **phonic knowledge** to write words in ways which match spoken sounds. ELG.		Distinguish between **homophones** and near homophones	Spell further **homophones**		Continue to distinguish between **homophones** and other words which are often confused.	
	Spell **days** of the week		Spell words that are often misspelt.*			
Some words are spelt correctly and others are **phonetically plausible**. ELG	Name the letters of the alphabet: - name in order - use letter names to distinguish between alternative spellings of same sound		Use the first two or three letters of a word to check its spelling in a **dictionary**		Use the first three or four letters of a word to check spelling, meaning or both of these in a **dictionary**. Use **dictionaries** to check the spelling and meaning of words. Use a **thesaurus**.	
Write some common **irregular** words. ELG	Add **prefixes & suffixes**: - -s or – es - un- - -ing, -ed, -er and –est (where no change is needed in the spelling of the root words)	Add **suffixes** to spell longer words: -ment, -ness, -ful, –less & -ly.	Use further **prefixes & suffixes** and understand how to add them.*		Use further **prefixes & suffixes** and understand the guidance for adding them	
	Write from memory simple sentences dictated by the teacher that include words using the GPCs and common exception words taught so far.	Write from memory simple sentences dictated by the teacher that include words using the GPCs, common exception words and punctuation taught so far.	Write **from memory** simple sentences, dictated by the teacher, that include taught words and punctuation taught so far.			
		Spell by learning the possessive apostrophe (singular).	Place the possessive apostrophe accurately in words with regular plurals and in words with irregular plurals.			
					Spell words with **silent letters**	
					Use knowledge of **morphology & etymology** in spelling and understand that the spelling of some words needs to be learnt specifically.*	

*See appendix 1 of National Curriculum for further detail.

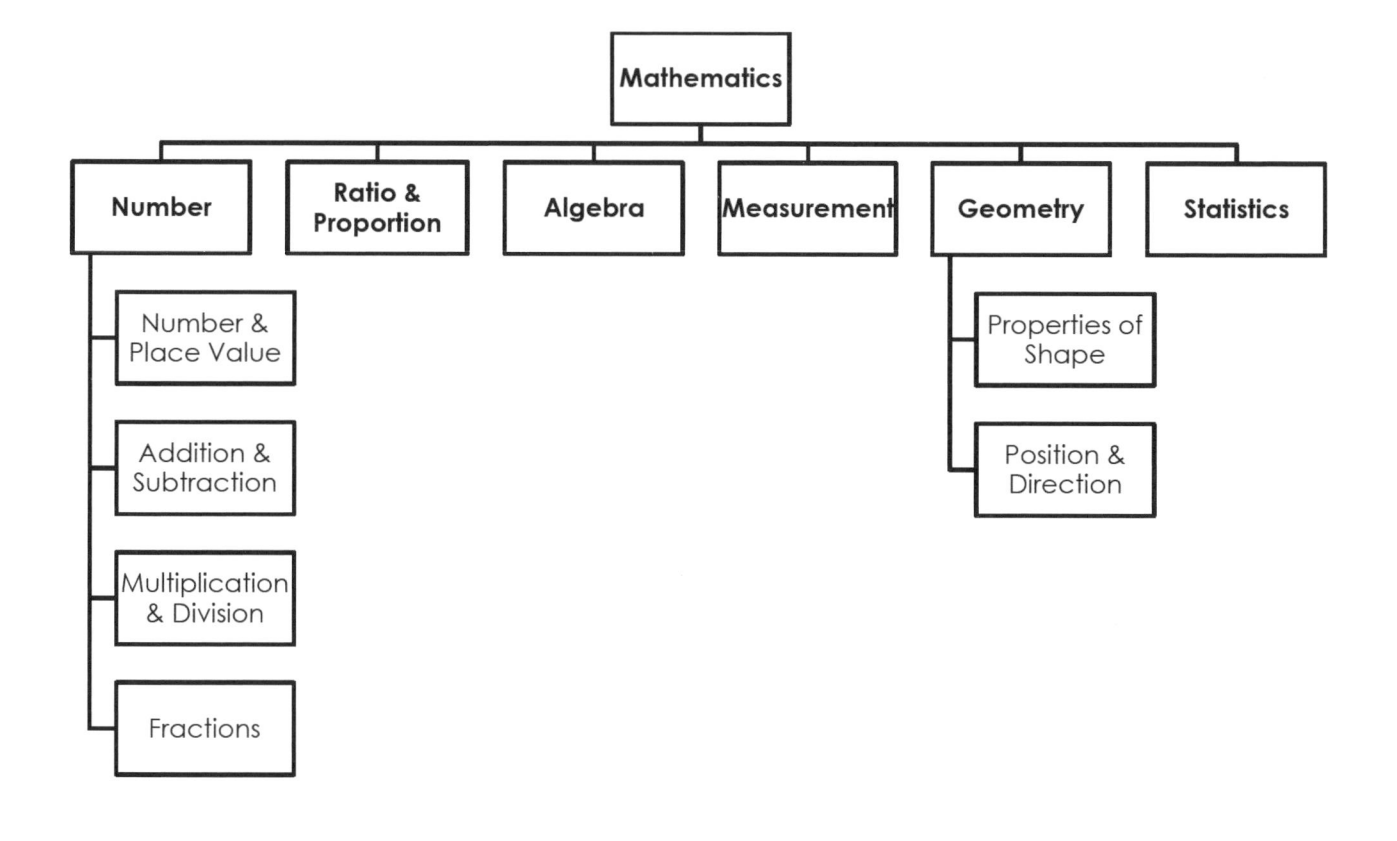

Number, place value & rounding

Rec/ELG	Y1	Y2	Y3	Y4	Y5	Y6
Count reliably with numbers from 1 – 20.	**Count** to and across 100, forward & backwards, beginning with 0 or 1, or from any given number.			**Count** backwards through zero to include negative numbers.	**Count** forwards or backwards in steps of powers of 10 for any given number up to 1 000 000.	
					Interpret **negative numbers** in context, count forwards and backwards with positive and negative whole numbers, including through zero.	Use **negative numbers** in context, & calculate intervals across zero.
	Count in **multiples** including 2s, 5s, and 10s.	Count in **steps** of 2, 3 & 5 from 0, and in tens from any number, forward & backward.	Count from 0 in **multiples** of 4, 8, 50 & 100.	Count in **multiples** of 6, 7, 9, 25 & 1000.		
Say which is 1 **more** or 1 **less** than a given number (to 20).	Given a number, identify 1 **more** & 1 **less**.		Find 10 or 100 **more** or **less** than a given number.	Find 1000 **more** or **less** than a given number.		
	Identify and represent numbers using concrete objects and pictorial representations including the number line, & use the language of: equal to, more than, less than (fewer), most, least.	**Identify, represent & estimate** numbers using different representations, incl the number line.	**Identify, represent & estimate** numbers using different representations.	**Identify, represent & estimate** numbers using different representations.		
	Read & write numbers to 100 in numerals. **Read & write** numbers from 1 – 20 in numerals & words	**Read & write** numbers to at least 100 in numerals and in words.	**Read & write** numbers to at least 1000 in numerals & in words.		**Read, write, order & compare** numbers to at least 1 000 000 & determine the value of each digit.	**Read, write, order & compare** numbers up to 10 000 000 & determine the value of each digit.
Order numbers 1 – 20.		**Compare & order** numbers from 0 up to 100; use <, > & = signs.	**Compare & order** numbers up to 1000.	**Compare & order** numbers beyond 1000.		
		Recognise the **place value** of each digit in a 2-digit number.	Recognise the **place value** of each digit in a 3-digit number.	Recognise the **place value** of each digit in a 4-digit number.	Read, write, order & compare numbers to at least 1 000 000 & determine the **value** of each digit.	
				Round any number to the nearest 10, 100 or 1000.	**Round** any number up to 1 000 000 to the nearest 10, 100, 1000, 10 000 & 100 000.	**Round** any whole number to a required degree of accuracy.
				Read **Roman numerals** to 100 (I to C) & understand that over time, the numeral system changed to include the concept of zero & place value.	Read **Roman numerals** to 1000 (M) and recognise years written in Roman numerals.	
		Use place value & number facts to **solve problems**.	Solve **number problems & practical problems** involving these ideas.	Solve **number & practical problems** that involve all of the above & with increasingly large positive numbers.	Solve **number & practical problems** that involve all of the above.	Solve **number & practical problems** that involve all of the above.

Addition and subtraction

Rec/ELG	Y1	Y2	Y3	Y4	Y5	Y6
	Read, write & interpret mathematical statements involving + - = signs.					
	Represent and use number bonds & related subtraction facts within 20.	**Recall** & use addition & subtraction facts to 20 fluently, & derive & use related facts up to 100.				
	Solve **one-step problems** that involve addition & subtraction, using concrete objects & pictorial representations, & missing number problems.	Solve **problems** with addition & subtraction: - Using concrete objects & pictorial representations, incl those involving numbers, quantities & measures - Applying their increasing knowledge of mental & written methods		Solve addition & subtraction **two-step problems** in contexts, deciding which operations & methods to use & why.	Solve addition & subtraction **multi-step problems** in contexts, deciding which operations & methods to use & why.	Solve addition & subtraction **multi-step problems** in contexts, deciding which operations & methods to use & why.
Add & subtract two single digit numbers. ELG Count on or back to find the answer. ELG	**Add & subtract** 1-digit & 2-digit numbers to 20, including zero.	**Add & subtract** numbers using concrete objects, pictorial representations, & mentally, including: - 2-digit no & ones - 2-digit no & tens - Two 2-digit numbers - Adding three 1-digit numbers	**Add & subtract** numbers mentally, including: - 3-digit no & ones - 3-digit no & tens - 3-digit no & hundreds		**Add & subtract** numbers mentally with increasingly large numbers.	Perform mental calculations, incl with **mixed operations** & large numbers.
			Add & subtract numbers with **up to 3 digits**, using formal written methods of columnar addition & subtraction.	**Add & subtract** numbers with **up to 4 digits** using the formal written methods of columnar addition & subtraction where appropriate.	**Add & subtract** whole numbers with more than 4 **digits** including using formal written methods (columnar addition & subtraction).	Use knowledge of the order of operations to carry out calculations involving **four operations**.
		Show that addition of two numbers can be done in any order (**commutative**) & subtraction of one number from another cannot.				
		Recognise & use the **inverse** relationship between addition & subtraction & use this to check calculations & missing number problems.	**Estimate** the answer to a calculation & use the **inverse** operations to check answers.	**Estimate** & use **inverse** operations to check answers to a calculation.	Use **rounding** to check answers to calculations & determine, in the context of a problem, levels of accuracy.	Use **estimation** to check answers to calculations & determine, in the context of a problem, levels of accuracy.
			Solve problems, incl missing number problems, number facts, place value, & more complex addition & subtraction.			**Solve problems** involving addition, subtraction, multiplication & division.

This page is intentionally blank

Multiplication and division						
Rec/ELG	Y1	Y2	Y3	Y4	Y5	Y6
		Recall & use multiplication & division facts for the **2, 5, 10 tables**, incl recognising odd & even nos.	Recall & use the **multiplication & division facts for the 3, 4, 8 tables**.	Recall **multiplication & division facts for tables up to 12x12**	Identify all **multiples & factors**, including finding all factor pairs of a number, & common factors of two numbers.	Identify **common factors, common multiples & prime numbers**.
					Know & use the **vocabulary of prime numbers, prime factors & composite** (non-prime) numbers.	
					Establish where a number up to 100 is **prime** & recall prime numbers up to 19.	
		Calculate the **mathematical statements** for multiplication & division within the multiplication tables & write them using x ÷ = signs.				
		Show that multiplication of two numbers can be done in any order (**commutative**) & division of one number by another cannot.		Recognise & use factor pairs & **commutativity** in mental calculations.		
					Multiply & divide numbers **mentally** drawing upon known facts.	Perform **mental** calculations, incl mixed operations & large numbers.
			Write & calculate mathematical statements for multiplication & division **using the multiplication tables** that they know, incl 2-digit x 1-digit, using mental & progressing to formal written methods.	**Multiply** 2-digit & 3-digit numbers by a 1-digit number using formal written layout.	**Multiply** numbers up to 4-digits by a 1-digit or 2-digit number using a formal written method, including long multiplication for 2-digit numbers.	**Multiply** multi-digit numbers up to 4-digits by a 2-digit whole number using the formal written method of **long multiplication**.
					Divide numbers up to 4-digits by a 1-digit number using the formal written method of short division & interpret remainders appropriately for the context.	**Divide** numbers up to 4-digits by a 2-digit whole number using the formal written method of **long division**, & interpret remainders as whole number remainders, fractions, or by rounding, as appropriate for the context.
						Divide numbers up to 4-digits by a 2-digit number using the formal written method of **short division** where appropriate, interpreting remainders according to the context.

					Use place value, known & derived facts to multiply & divide mentally, including **multiplying by 0 and 1; dividing by 1**; multiplying three numbers together.	**Multiply & divide** whole numbers & those involving decimals **by 10, 100 and 1000.**	
						Recognise & use **square numbers & cube numbers**, & the notation for squared [2] and cubed [3].	
Solve problems, including doubling, halving & sharing. ELG	Solve **one-step problems** involving multiplication & division, calculating the answer using concrete objects, pictorial representations & arrays with the support of the teacher.	Solve **problems** involving multiplication & division, using materials, arrays, repeated addition, mental methods, & multiplication & division facts, incl problems in context.	Solve **problems**, incl missing number problems, involving multiplication & division, incl integer scaling problems & correspondence problems in which n objects are connected to m objects.	**Solve problems** involving multiplying and adding, including the distributive law to multiply 2-digit numbers by 1-digit, integer scaling problems & harder multiplication problems such as n objects are connected to m objects.	**Solve problems** involving addition, subtractions, multiplication & division & a combination of these, incl understanding the meaning of the equals sign.	Use knowledge of the order of operations to carry out calculations involving **four operations.**
						Solve problems involving multiplication & division, including scaling by simple fractions & problems involving simple rates.	**Solve problems** involving addition, subtraction, multiplication & division.
						Solve problems involving multiplication & division including using their knowledge of factors & multiples, squares and cubes.	

Fractions, decimals and percentages

Rec/ELG	Y1	Y2	Y3	Y4	Y5	Y6
						Associate a fraction with division & calculate decimal fraction equivalents (e.g. 0.375) for a simple fraction (e.g. 3/8).
Solve problems, including **doubling, halving & sharing.** ELG	Recognise, find & name a **half** as one of two equal parts of an object, shape or quantity. Recognise, find & name a **quarter** as one of four equal parts of an object, shape or quantity.	Recognise, find, name & write fractions **1/3, 1/4, 2/4,** and **3/4** or a length, shape, set of objects or quantity.		Recognise & show, using diagrams, families of common **equivalent fractions.** Recognise & write **decimal equivalents** on any number of tenths or hundredths. Recognise & write **decimal equivalents** to ¼, ½, ¾.	Identify, name & write **equivalent fractions** of a given fraction, represented visually, incl tenths & hundredths. **Read & write decimal numbers** as fractions (e.g. 0.71 = 71/100).	Identify the **value of each digit to three decimal places** and multiply & divide numbers by 10, 100 and 1000 where the answers are up to three decimal places
				Find the effect of dividing a 1-digit or 2-digit number by 10 and 100, identifying the value of the digits in the answer as units, tenths and hundredths.		
		Write simple fractions, e.g. ½ or 6 =3 and recognise the **equivalence** of 2/4 & 1/2.	**Count up & down** in tenths; recognise that tenths arise from dividing an object into 10 equal parts & in dividing 1-digit numbers or quantities by 10.	**Count up & down** in hundredths; recognise that hundredths arise when dividing an object by a hundred & dividing tenths by ten.	**Recognise & use thousandths** & relate then to tenths, hundredths & decimal equivalents.	
					Recognise mixed numbers & improper fractions & convert from one form to the other & write mathematical statements.	
			Compare & order unit fractions, & fractions with the same denominators.		**Compare & order** fractions whose denominators are all multiples of the same number.	**Compare & order fractions**, including fractions >1. Use common factors to simplify fractions; use common multiples to express fractions in the same denomination
			Recognise, find & write fractions or a discrete set of objects: unit fractions & non-unit fractions with small denominators			
			Recognise & use fractions as numbers: unit fractions & non-unit fractions with small denominators.			
			Recognise & show, using diagrams, equivalent fractions with small denominators.			

				Add & subtract fractions with the same denominator within one whole (e.g. 5/7+1/7=6/7)	Add & subtract fractions with the same denominator.	Add & subtract fractions with the same denominator & multiples of the same number.	Add & subtract fractions with different denominators & mixed numbers, using the concept of equivalent fractions.
						Multiply proper fractions & mixed numbers by whole numbers, supported by materials & diagrams.	**Multiply** simple pairs of proper fractions, writing the answer in its simplest form (e.g. ¼ x ½ = 1/8)
							Multiply 1-digit numbers with up to two decimal places by whole numbers.
							Divide proper fractions by whole numbers (e.g. 1/3 ÷ 2 = 1/6). Use written division methods in cases where the answer has up to two decimal places.
					Round decimals with one decimal place to the nearest whole number.	**Round decimals** with two decimal places to the nearest whole number and to one decimal place.	
					Compare numbers with the same number of decimal places up to **two decimal places**.	Read, write, order and **compare numbers** with up to **three decimal places**.	
						Recognise the **per cent symbol** (%) & understand that per cent relates to 'number or parts per hundred', and write percentages as a fraction with denominator hundred, and as a decimal fraction.	
							Recall & use **equivalences** between simple fractions, decimals & percentages, including in different contexts.
						Solve problems which require knowing **percentage & decimal equivalents** of ½, ¼, 1/5, 2/5, 4/5 and those with a denominator of a multiple of 10 or 25.	Solve problems involving the **calculation of percentages** of whole numbers or measures such as 15% of 360 and the use of percentages for comparison.*
				Solve problems that involve all of the above.	**Solve problems** involving increasingly harder fractions to calculate quantities, & fractions to divide quantities, including non-unit fractions where the answer is a whole number. Solve simple measure & money problems involving fractions & decimals to two decimal places.	**Solve problems** involving number up to three decimal places.	**Solve problems** which require answers to be rounded to specified degrees of accuracy.

* Extract from proportion section of NC

Algebra

Rec/ELG	Y1	Y2	Y3	Y4	Y5	Y6
Express missing number problems algebraically.						
Use simple formulae						
Generate & describe linear number sequences.						
Find pairs of numbers that satisfy an equation with two unknowns.						
Enumerate all possibilities of combinations of two variables.						

Ratio and proportion

Rec/ELG	Y1	Y2	Y3	Y4	Y5	Y6
Solve problems involving the **relative sizes** of two quantities where missing values can be found by using integer multiplication & division facts.						
Solve problems involving the **calculation of percentages** of whole numbers or measures such as 15% of 360 and the use of percentages for comparison.						
Solve problems involving similar shapes where the scale factor is known or can be found.						
Solve problems involving **unequal sharing & grouping** using knowledge of fractions & multiples.						

This page is intentionally blank

Measurement

Rec/ELG	Y1	Y2	Y3	Y4	Y5	Y6
GENERAL Use everyday language to talk about size, weight, capacity, position, distance, time & money to compare quantities and objects and solve problems. ELG	Compare, describe & solve practical problems for: - Lengths & heights - Mass/weight - Capacity & volume - Time Measure & begin to record the following: - Length & heights - Mass/weight - Capacity & volume - Time (hrs, mins, secs)	Choose and use appropriate standard units to estimate and measure: - length/height in any direction (m/cm) - mass (kg/g) - temperature (°C) - capacity (l/ml) to the nearest appropriate unit, using rulers, scales, thermometers & measuring vessels. Compare & order lengths, mass, volume/capacity & record the results using >, < and =.	Measure, compare, add & subtract: - lengths (m/cm/mm) - mass (kg/g) - volume/capacity (l/ml)	Convert between different units of measure (e.g. km to m; hr to min) Estimate, compare & calculate different measures.	Convert between different units of metric measure (e.g. km/m; cm/m; cm/mm; g/kg; l/ml). Understand & use approximate equivalences between metric units & common imperial units such as inches, pounds & pints. Use all four operations to solve problems involving measure using decimal notation, including scaling. Estimate volume (e.g. using 1 cm³ blocks to build cubes & cuboids) & capacity (e.g. using water).	Solve problems involving the calculation & conversion of units of measure, using decimal notation to three decimal places where appropriate. Use, read, write & convert between standard units, converting measurements of length, mass, volume & time from a smaller unit of measure to a larger unit, and vice versa, using decimal notation to three decimal places. Calculate, estimate & compare volume of cubes & cuboids using standard units, incl cm³ and m³, and extending to other units such as mm³ and km³. Convert between miles & km. Recognise when it is possible to use the formulae for area & volume of shapes.
PERIMETER			Measure the **perimeter** of simple 2D shapes.	Measure & calculate the **perimeter** of a rectilinear figure (incl squares) in cm & m.	Measure & calculate the **perimeter** of composite rectilinear shapes in cm & m.	Recognise that shapes with the same areas can have different **perimeters** & vice versa.
AREA				Find the **area** of rectilinear shapes by counting squares.	Calculate & compare the **area** of rectangles (including squares, & including using standard units, square centimetres (cm²) and square metres (m²) & estimate the area of irregular shapes.	Calculate the **area** of parallelograms & triangles. Recognise when it is possible to use the formulae for **area** & volume of shapes.

MONEY	Recognise & know the value of different **denominations** or coins & notes.	Recognise & use symbols for **pounds** (£) and **pence** (p); combine amounts to make a particular value. Find different combinations of coins that equal the same amounts of money. Solve simple problems in a practical context involving addition & subtraction of money of the same unit, incl giving change.	**Add & subtract amounts** of money to give change, using both £ and p in practical contexts.	Estimate, compare & **calculate** different measures, including money in pounds & pence.		
TIME	Sequence events in **chronological order** using language (e.g. before, after, next, first, today, yesterday, tomorrow, morning, afternoon, evening). Recognise & use **language** relating to dates, incl days of the week, weeks, months, years. **Tell the time to the hour & half past the hour** & draw the hands on a clock face to show these times.	Compare & **sequence** intervals of time. Tell & write the time to **five minutes**, incl **quarter past/to** the hour & draw the hands on a clock face to show these times.	Tell & write the time from an analogue clock, incl using **Roman numerals** from I to XII, & **12-hour & 24-hour** clocks. Estimate & read **time with increasing accuracy to the nearest minute**; record & compare time in terms of secs, mins, hrs; use vocabulary such as o'clock, am/pm, morning, afternoon, noon & midnight. Know the numbers of **seconds in a minute** & the number of **days each month, year & leap year**. **Compare durations** of events, for example to calculate time taken by particular events or tasks.	**Read, write & convert time** between analogue & digital 12- & 24-hour clocks. Solve problems involving **converting** from hours to minutes; minutes to seconds; years to months; weeks to days.	Solve problems involving **converting** between units of time.		

Geometry: properties of shapes

Rec/ELG	Y1	Y2	Y3	Y4	Y5	Y6
Explore the characteristics of everyday objects & shapes and use mathematical language to describe them. ELG	**Recognise & name common 2D & 3D shapes**, including: - 2D, e.g. rectangles (including squares), circles, triangles - 3D, e.g. cuboids (including cubes), pyramids, spheres.	**Identify & describe the properties of 2D shapes**, incl the number of sides & symmetry in a vertical line. **Identify & describe the properties of 3D shapes**, incl the number of edges, vertices & faces. Identify 2D shapes on the surface of 3D shapes. **Compare & sort** common 2D & 3D shapes & everyday objects.	**Draw 2D shapes & make 3D** shapes using modelling materials; recognise 3D shapes in different orientations; & describe them. Recognise **angles** are a property of shape or a description of a turn. Identify **right angles**, recognise that two right angles make a half-turn, three make three quarters of a complete turn; identify whether angles are greater than or less than a right angle.	**Compare & classify** geometric shapes, incl quadrilaterals and triangles, based on their properties & sizes. Identify lines of **symmetry** in 2D shapes presented in different orientations. Complete a simple **symmetric figure** with respect to a specific line of symmetry. Identify acute & obtuse **angles & compare & order** angles up to two right angles by size.	**Identify 3D shapes,** including cubes & cuboids, from 2D representations. Use the **properties of rectangles to** deduce related facts & find missing lengths & angles. Distinguish between **regular & irregular polygons** based on reasoning about equal sides & angles. Know **angles** are measures in degrees; estimate & compare acute, obtuse & reflex angles. Draw given angles, & measure them in degrees.	**Draw 2D shapes** using given dimensions & angles. **Recognise, describe & build simple 3D shapes,** incl making nets. **Compare & classify** geometric shapes based on their properties & sizes & find unknown angles in any triangles, quadrilaterals, & regular polygons. Recognise **angles** where they meet at a point, are on a straight line, or are vertically opposite, & find missing angles.
			Identify horizontal and vertical lines and pairs of perpendicular & parallel lines.		Identify: - Angles at a point on a straight line & ½ a turn (total 180°) - Angles at a point & one whole turn (total 360°) - Other multiples of 90°	Illustrate & name parts of **circles,** including radius, diameter & circumference & know that the diameter is twice the radius.

Geometry: position, direction, motion

Rec/ELG	Y1	Y2	Y3	Y4	Y5	Y6
Recognise, create & describe patterns. ELG		**Order & arrange** combinations of mathematical objects in patterns and sequences.				
	Describe **position, directions & movement**, including half, quarter and three-quarter turns.	Use mathematical vocabulary to describe **position, direction & movement**, including movement in a straight line and distinguishing between rotation as a turn & in terms of right angles for quarter, half and three-quarter turns (clockwise & anti-clockwise).				
				Describe positions on a 2D grid as **coordinates in the first quadrant**.		Describe positions on the full coordinate grid (**all four quadrants**).
				Describe movements between positions as **translations** of a given unit to the left/right and up/down.	Identify, describe & represent the position of a shape following a **reflection or translation**, using the appropriate language, & know that the shape has not changed.	**Draw & translate simple shapes** on the coordinate plane, & reflect them in the axes.
				Plot specified points & draw sides to complete a given polygon.		

Statistics

Rec/ELG	Y1	Y2	Y3	Y4	Y5	Y6
		Interpret & construct simple: - **pictograms** - **tally charts** - **block diagrams** - **simple tables**	Interpret & present data using: - **bar charts** - **pictograms** - **tables**	Interpret & present discrete data using appropriate graphical methods, incl: - **bar charts** - **time graphs**	Complete, read & interpret information in: - **tables, incl timetables**	Interpret & construct: - **pie charts** - **line graphs** and use to solve problems.
		Ask & answer simple questions by counting the number of objects in each category & sorting the categories by quantity. **Ask & answer** questions about totalling and compare categorical data.	Solve one-**step & two-step questions** such as 'How many more?' and 'How many fewer?' using information presented in scaled bar charts & pictograms & tables.	Solve **comparison, sum & difference problems** using information presented in bar charts, pictograms, tables & other graphs.	Solve **comparison, sum & difference problems** using information presented in a line graph.	Calculate & interpret the **mean** as an average.

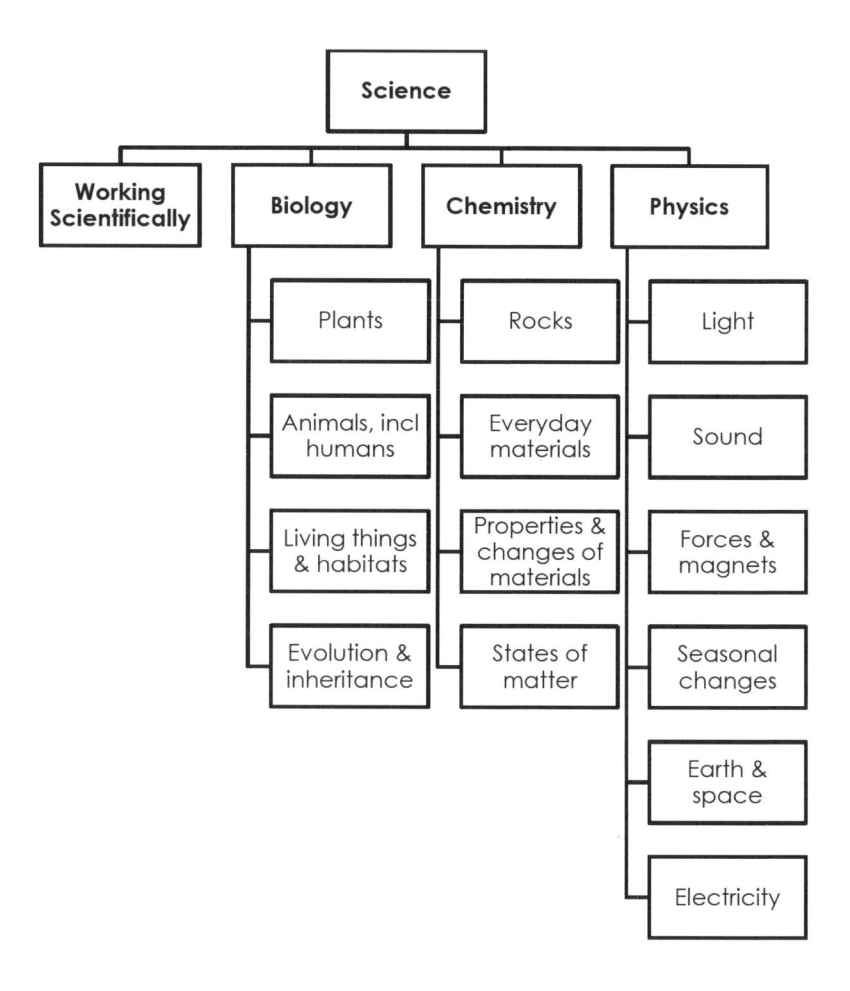

	Biology				Chemistry				Physics					
	Plants	Animals, including humans	Living things & habitats	Evolution & inheritance	Rocks	Everyday materials	Properties & changes of materials	States of matter	Light	Sound	Forces & magnets	Seasonal changes	Earth & space	Electricity
Yr 1	X	X				X						X		
Yr 2	X	X	X			X								
Yr 3	X	X			X				X		X			
Yr 4		X	X					X		X				X
Yr 5		X	X				X		X		X		X	
Yr 6		X	X	X										X

Unit:	Y1	Y2	Y3	Y4	Y5	Y6
Working scientifically (taught throughout each unit)	Yes	Yes	Yes	Yes	Yes	Yes

Years 1 and 2	Years 3 and 4	Years 5 and 6
Asking simple **questions** and recognising that they can be answered in different ways	Asking relevant **questions** and using different types of scientific enquiries to answer them	Planning different types of scientific enquiries to answer **questions**, including recognising and controlling variables where necessary
	Using straightforward **scientific evidence** to answer questions or to support their findings	Identifying **scientific evidence** that has been used to support or refute ideas or arguments
Observing closely, using simple equipment	Making systematic and careful **observations** and, where appropriate, taking accurate **measurements** using standard units, using a range of equipment, including thermometers and data loggers	Taking **measurements**, using a range of scientific equipment, with increasing accuracy and precision, taking repeat readings where necessary
Performing simple **tests**	Setting up simple practical **enquiries**, comparative and **fair tests**	
Identifying and **classifying**	**Identifying** differences, similarities or changes related to simple scientific ideas and processes.	
Using their observations and ideas to suggest answers to questions	**Using results** to draw simple conclusions, make predictions for new values, suggest improvements and raise further questions	**Using test results** to make predictions to set up further comparative and fair tests
Gathering and **recording** data to help in answering questions	**Recording** findings using simple scientific language, drawings, labelled diagrams, keys, bar charts, and tables	**Recording** data and results of increasing complexity using scientific diagrams and labels, classification keys, tables, and bar and line graphs
	Gathering, recording, classifying and presenting **data** in a variety of ways to help in answering questions	
	Reporting on findings from enquiries, including oral and written explanations, displays or presentations of results and conclusions	**Reporting** and **presenting** findings from enquiries, including conclusions, causal relationships and explanations of and degree of trust in results, in oral and written forms such as displays and other presentations
*Pupils should read and spell scientific **vocabulary** at a level consistent with their increasing word and spelling knowledge at key stage 1.*	*Pupils should read & spell scientific **vocabulary** correctly & with confidence, using their growing word reading & spelling knowledge.*	*Pupils should read, spell & pronounce scientific **vocabulary** correctly.*

Unit:	Y1	Y2	Y3	Y4	Y5	Y6
Plants	Yes	Yes	Yes	-	-	-

Year 1	Year 2	Year 3
▪ Identify and **name a variety of common wild & garden plants**, including deciduous and evergreen trees. ▪ Identify and describe the basic **structure** of a variety of common flowering plants, including trees.	▪ Observe and describe **how seeds and bulbs grow** into mature plants. ▪ Find out and describe how **plants need** water, light and a suitable temperature to grow and stay healthy.	▪ Identify and describe the **functions** of different parts of flowering plants: roots, stem/trunk, leaves and flowers. ▪ Explore the requirements of plants for life & growth (air, light, water, nutrients from soil, & room to grow) & how they vary from plant to plant. ▪ Investigate the way in which **water is transported** within plants. ▪ Explore the **part that flowers play** in the life cycle of a flowering plant, including pollination, seed formation and seed dispersal.

Unit:					Y1	Y2	Y3	Y4	Y5	Y6
Animals, including humans					Yes	Yes	Yes	Yes	Yes	Yes

Year 1	Year 2	Year 3	Year 4	Year 5	Year 6
<ul><li>**Identify and name** a variety of common animals including fish, amphibians, reptiles, birds & mammals.</li><li>**Identify and name** a variety of common animals that are carnivores, herbivores and omnivores.</li><li>Describe and compare the **structure** of a variety of common animals (fish, amphibians, reptiles, birds & mammals, including pets).</li></ul>	<ul><li>Notice that animals, including humans, have **offspring** which grow into adults.</li><li>Find out about and describe the **basic needs of animals**, including humans, for survival (water, food and air).</li></ul>	<ul><li>Identify that animals, including humans, need the right types and amount of **nutrition**, and that they cannot make their own food; they get nutrition from what they eat</li></ul>	<ul><li>Construct and interpret a variety of **food chains**, identifying producers, predators and prey.</li></ul>		<ul><li>Describe the ways in which **nutrients** and water are transported within animals, including humans.</li></ul>

▪ Identify, name, draw and label the basic parts of the **human body** and say which part of the body is associated with each sense.	▪ Describe the importance for **humans** of exercise, eating the right amounts of different types of food, and hygiene.	▪ Identify that **humans** and some animals have skeletons and muscles for support, protection and movement.	▪ Describe the simple functions of the basic parts of the **digestive system** in humans. ▪ Identify the different types of **teeth** in humans and their simple functions	▪ Describe the **changes as humans develop** from birth to old age.	▪ Identify and name the main parts of the **human circulatory system**, and describe the functions of the heart, blood vessels and blood. ▪ Recognise the **impact of diet, exercise, drugs and lifestyle** on the way their bodies function

Unit:			Y1	Y2	Y3	Y4	Y5	Y6
Living things and habitats			-	Yes	-	Yes	Yes	Yes

Year 2	Year 4	Year 5	Year 6
<ul><li>Explore and compare the differences between things that are **living, dead, and things that have never been alive**.</li><li>Identify that most living things live in **habitats** to which they are suited and describe how different habitats provide for the basic needs of different kinds of animals and plants, and how they depend on each other.</li><li>**Identify and name a variety of plants and animals** in their habitats, including micro-habitats.</li><li>Describe **how animals obtain their food** from plants and other animals, using the idea of a simple **food chain**, and identify and name different sources of food.</li></ul>	<ul><li>Recognise that living things can be grouped in a variety of ways.</li><li>Explore and use classification keys to help group, identify & name a variety of living things in their local & wider environment.</li><li>Recognise that **environments can change** and that this can sometimes pose dangers to living things.</li></ul>	<ul><li>Describe the differences in the **life cycles** of a mammal, an amphibian, an insect and a bird.</li><li>Describe the life process of **reproduction** in some plants and animals.</li></ul>	<ul><li>Describe how living things are **classified** into broad groups according to common observable characteristics and based on similarities and differences, including micro-organisms, plants and animals.</li><li>Give reasons for **classifying** plants and animals based on specific characteristics.</li></ul>

Unit:	Y1	Y2	Y3	Y4	Y5	Y6
Evolution and inheritance	-	-	-	-	-	Yes

Year 6
- Recognise that living things have changed over time and that fossils provide information about living things that inhabited the Earth millions of years ago.
- Recognise that living things produce offspring of the same kind, but normally offspring vary and are not identical to their parents.
- Identify how animals and plants are adapted to suit their environment in different ways and that adaptation may lead to evolution.

Unit:	Y1	Y2	Y3	Y4	Y5	Y6
Rocks	-	-	Yes	-	-	-

Year 3
- Compare and group together different kinds of rocks on the basis of their appearance and simple physical properties.
- Describe in simple terms how fossils are formed when things that have lived are trapped within rock.
- Recognise that soils are made from rocks and organic matter.

Unit:	Y1	Y2	Y3	Y4	Y5	Y6
Everyday materials	Yes	Yes	-	-	-	-

Year 1	Year 2
<ul><li>Distinguish between an **object and the material** from which it is made.</li><li>**Identify and name** a variety of everyday materials, including wood, plastic, glass, metal, water, and rock.</li><li>Describe the simple **physical properties** of a variety of everyday materials.</li><li>**Compare and group** together a variety of everyday materials on the basis of their simple physical properties.</li></ul>	<ul><li>Identify and **compare the suitability** of a variety of everyday materials, including wood, metal, plastic, glass, brick, rock, paper and cardboard for particular uses.</li><li>Find out how the shapes of solid objects made from some materials can be changes by squashing, bending, twisting & stretching.</li></ul>

Unit:	Y1	Y2	Y3	Y4	Y5	Y6
Properties and changes of materials	-	-	-	-	Yes	-

Year 5

- Compare and group together everyday materials on the basis of their properties, including their hardness, solubility, transparency, conductivity (electrical and thermal), and response to magnets.
- Know that some materials will dissolve in liquid to form a solution, and describe how to recover a substance from a solution.
- Use knowledge of solids, liquids and gases to decide how mixtures might be separated, including through filtering, sieving and evaporating.
- Give reasons, based on evidence from comparative and fair tests, for the particular uses of everyday materials, including metals, wood and plastic.
- Demonstrate that dissolving, mixing and changes of state are reversible changes.
- Explain that some changes result in the formation of new materials, and that this kind of change is not usually reversible, including changes associated with burning and the action of acid on bicarbonate of soda.

Unit:		Y1	Y2	Y3	Y4	Y5	Y6
States of matter		-	-	-	Yes	-	-

Year 4
- Compare and group materials together, according to whether they are solids, liquids or gases.
- Observe that some materials change state when they are heated or cooled, and measure or research the temperature at which this happens in degrees Celsius (°C).
- Identify the part played by evaporation and condensation in the water cycle and associate the rate of evaporation with temperature.

Unit:		Y1	Y2	Y3	Y4	Y5	Y6
Light		-	-	Yes	-	Yes	-

Year 3	**Year 5**
- Recognise that they need light in order to see things and that dark is the absence of light. - Notice that light is reflected from surfaces. - Recognise that light from the sun can be dangerous and that there are ways to protect their eyes. - Recognise that shadows are formed when the light from a light source is blocked by a solid object. - Find patterns in the way that the size of shadows change.	- Recognise that light appears to travel in straight lines. - Use the idea that light travels in straight lines to explain that objects are seen because they give out or reflect light into the eye. - Explain that we see things because light travels from light sources to our eyes or from light sources to objects and then to our eyes. - Use the idea that light travels in straight lines to explain why shadows have the same shape as the objects that cast them.

Unit:		Y1	Y2	Y3	Y4	Y5	Y6
Sound		-	-	-	Yes	-	-

Year 4
- Identify how sounds are made, associating some of them with something vibrating.
- Recognise that vibrations from sounds travel through a medium to the ear.
- Find patterns between the pitch of a sound and features of the object that produced it.
- Find patterns between the volume of a sound and the strength of the vibrations that produced it.
- Recognise that sounds get fainter as the distance from the sound increases.

Unit:	Y1	Y2	Y3	Y4	Y5	Y6
Forces and magnets	-	-	Yes	-	Yes	-

Year 3	Year 5
<ul><li>Compare how things move on different surfaces.</li><li>Notice that some forces need contact between two objects, but magnetic forces can act at a distance.</li><li>Observe how magnets attract or repel each other and attract some materials and not others.</li><li>Compare and group together a variety of everyday materials on the basis of whether they are attracted to a magnet, and identify some magnetic materials.</li><li>Describe magnets as having two poles.</li><li>Predict whether two magnets will attract or repel each other, depending on which poles are facing.</li></ul>	<ul><li>Explain that unsupported objects fall towards the Earth because of the force of gravity acting between the Earth and the falling object.</li><li>Identify the effects of air resistance, water resistance and friction that act between moving surfaces.</li><li>Recognise that some mechanisms, including levers, pulleys and gears, allow a smaller force to have greater effect.</li></ul>

Unit:	Y1	Y2	Y3	Y4	Y5	Y6
Seasonal changes	Yes	-	-	-	-	-

Year 1

- Observe changes across the four seasons.
- Observe and describe weather associated with the seasons and how day length varies.

Unit:	Y1	Y2	Y3	Y4	Y5	Y6
Earth and space	-	-	-	-	Yes	-

Year 5

- Describe the movement of the Earth, and other planets, relative to the Sun in the solar system.
- Describe the movement of the Moon relative to the Earth.
- Describe the Sun, Earth and Moon as approximately spherical bodies.
- Use the idea of the Earth's rotation to explain day and night and the apparent movement of the sun across the sky.

Unit:				Y1	Y2	Y3	Y4	Y5	Y6
Electricity				-	-	-	Yes	-	Yes

Year 4	Year 6
<ul><li>Identify common appliances that run on electricity.</li><li>Construct a simple series electrical circuit, identifying and naming its basic parts, including cells, wires, bulbs, switches and buzzers.</li><li>Identify whether or not a lamp will light in a simple series circuit, based on whether or not the lamp is part of a complete loop with a battery.</li><li>Recognise that a switch opens and closes a circuit and associate this with whether or not a lamp lights in a simple series circuit.</li><li>Recognise some common conductors and insulators, and associate metals with being good conductors.</li></ul>	<ul><li>Associate the brightness of a lamp or the volume of a buzzer with the number and voltage of cells used in the circuit.</li><li>Compare and give reasons for variations in how components function, including the brightness of bulbs, the loudness of buzzers and the on/off position of switches.</li><li>Use recognised symbols when representing a simple circuit in a diagram.</li></ul>

This page is intentionally blank

Art	
KS1	Pupils should be taught: • to use a range of materials creatively to design and make products • to use drawing, painting and sculpture to develop and share their ideas, experiences and imagination • to develop a wide range of art and design techniques in using colour, pattern, texture, line, shape, form and space • about the work of a range of artists, craft makers and designers, describing the differences and similarities between different practices and disciplines, and making links to their own work
KS2	Pupils should be taught to develop their techniques, including their control and their use of materials, with creativity, experimentation and an increasing awareness of different kinds of art, craft and design. Pupils should be taught: • to create sketch books to record their observations and use them to review and revisit ideas • to improve their mastery of art and design techniques, including drawing, painting and sculpture with a range of materials (e.g. pencil, charcoal, paint, clay) • about great artists, architects and designers in history.

Computing	
KS1	Pupils should be taught to: • understand what algorithms are; how they are implemented as programs on digital devices; and that programs execute by following precise and unambiguous instructions • create and debug simple programs • use logical reasoning to predict the behaviour of simple programs • use technology purposefully to create, organise, store, manipulate and retrieve digital content • recognise common uses of information technology beyond school • use technology safely and respectfully, keeping personal information private; identify where to go for help and support when they have concerns about content or contact on the internet or other online technologies
KS2	Pupils should be taught to: • design, write and debug programs that accomplish specific goals, including controlling or simulating physical systems; solve problems by decomposing them into smaller parts • use sequence, selection, and repetition in programs; work with variables and various forms of input and output • use logical reasoning to explain how some simple algorithms work and to detect and correct errors in algorithms and programs • understand computer networks including the internet; how they can provide multiple services, such as the world-wide web; and the opportunities they offer for communication and collaboration • use search technologies effectively, appreciate how results are selected and ranked, and be discerning in evaluating digital content • select, use and combine a variety of software (including internet services) on a range of digital devices to design & create a range of programs, systems and content that accomplish given goals, including collecting, analysing, evaluating and presenting data and information • use technology safely, respectfully and responsibly; recognise acceptable/unacceptable behaviour; identify a range of ways to report concerns about content and contact

Design and technology	
KS1	Through a variety of creative and practical activities, pupils should be taught the knowledge, understanding and skills needed to engage in an iterative process of designing and making. They should work in a range of relevant contexts (e.g. the home and school, gardens and playgrounds, the local community, industry and the wider environment). When designing and making, pupils should be taught to:

Design	Make	Evaluate	Technical knowledge
▪ design purposeful, functional, appealing products for themselves and other users based on design criteria ▪ generate, develop, model and communicate their ideas through talking, drawing, templates, mock-ups and, where appropriate, information and communication technology	▪ select from and use a range of tools and equipment to perform practical tasks, e.g. cutting, shaping, joining and finishing ▪ select from and use a wide range of materials and components, including construction materials, textiles and ingredients, according to their characteristics	▪ explore and evaluate a range of existing products ▪ evaluate their ideas and products against design criteria	▪ build structures, exploring how they can be made stronger, stiffer and more stable ▪ explore and use mechanisms (e.g. levers, sliders, wheels and axles), in their products

Cooking and nutrition
- use the basic principles of a healthy and varied diet to prepare dishes
- understand where food comes from

KS2	Through a variety of creative and practical activities, pupils should be taught the knowledge, understanding and skills needed to engage in an iterative process of designing and making. They should work in a range of relevant contexts (e.g. the home, school, leisure, culture, enterprise, industry and the wider environment). When designing and making, pupils should be taught to:

Design	Make	Evaluate	Technical knowledge
▪ use research and develop design criteria to inform the design of innovative, functional, appealing products that are fit for purpose, aimed at particular individuals or groups ▪ generate, develop, model and communicate their ideas through discussion, annotated sketches, cross-sectional and exploded diagrams, prototypes, pattern pieces and computer-aided design	▪ select from and use a wider range of tools and equipment to perform practical tasks (e.g. cutting, shaping, joining and finishing), accurately ▪ select from and use a wider range of materials and components, including construction materials, textiles and ingredients, according to their functional properties and aesthetic qualities	▪ investigate and analyse a range of existing products ▪ evaluate their ideas and products against their own design criteria and consider the views of others to improve their work ▪ understand how key events and individuals in design and technology have helped shape the world	▪ apply their understanding of how to strengthen, stiffen and reinforce more complex structures ▪ understand and use mechanical systems in their products (e.g. gears, pulleys, cams, levers and linkages) ▪ understand and use electrical systems in their products (e.g. series circuits incorporating switches, bulbs, buzzers and motors) ▪ apply their understanding of computing to program, monitor and control their products.

Cooking and nutrition
- ▪ understand and apply the principles of a healthy and varied diet
- ▪ prepare and cook a variety of predominantly savoury dishes using a range of cooking techniques
- ▪ understand seasonality, and know where and how a variety of ingredients are grown, reared, caught and processed.

Geography	
KS1	Pupils should develop knowledge about the world, the United Kingdom and their locality. They should understand basic subject-specific vocabulary relating to human and physical geography and begin to use geographical skills, including first-hand observation, to enhance their locational awareness. Pupils should be taught to:

Location knowledge	Place knowledge	Human and physical geography	Geographical skills and fieldwork

▪ name and locate the world's seven continents and five oceans
▪ name, locate and identify characteristics of the four countries and capital cities of the United Kingdom and its surrounding seas
	▪ understand geographical similarities and differences through studying the human and physical geography of a small area of the United Kingdom, and of a small area in a contrasting non-European country	▪ identify seasonal and daily weather patterns in the United Kingdom and the location of hot and cold areas of the world in relation to the Equator and the North and South Poles
		▪ use basic geographical vocabulary to refer to:
		  ○ key physical features, including: beach, cliff, coast, forest, hill, mountain, sea, ocean, river, soil, valley, vegetation, season and weather
		  ○ key human features, including: city, town, village, factory, farm, house, office, port, harbour and shop
			▪ use world maps, atlases and globes to identify the United Kingdom and its countries, as well as the countries, continents and oceans studied at this key stage
			▪ use simple compass directions (North, South, East and West) and locational and directional language (e.g. near and far; left and right) to describe the location of features and routes on a map
			▪ use aerial photographs and plan perspectives to recognise landmarks and basic human and physical features; devise a simple map; and use and construct basic symbols in a key
			▪ use simple fieldwork and observational skills to study the geography of their school and its grounds and the key human and physical features of its surrounding environment

Geography				
KS2	Pupils should extend their knowledge and understanding beyond the local area to include the United Kingdom and Europe, North and South America. This will include the location and characteristics of a range of the world's most significant human and physical features. They should develop their use of geographical tools and skills to enhance their locational and place knowledge. Pupils should be taught to:			
	Location knowledge	Place knowledge	Human and physical geography	Geographical skills and fieldwork
	<ul><li>locate the world's countries, using maps to focus on Europe (including the location of Russia) and North and South America, concentrating on their environmental regions, key physical and human characteristics, countries, and major cities</li><li>name and locate counties and cities of the United Kingdom, geographical regions and their identifying human and physical characteristics, key topographical features (including hills, mountains, coasts and rivers), and land-use patterns; and understand how some of these aspects have changed over time</li><li>identify the position and significance of latitude, longitude, Equator, Northern Hemisphere, Southern Hemisphere, the Tropics of Cancer and Capricorn, Arctic and Antarctic Circle, the Prime/Greenwich Meridian and time zones (including day and night)</li></ul>	<ul><li>understand geographical similarities and differences through the study of human and physical geography of a region of the United Kingdom, a region in a European country, and a region within North or South America</li></ul>	<ul><li>describe and understand key aspects of:<ul><li>physical geography, including: climate zones, biomes and vegetation belts, rivers, mountains, volcanoes and earthquakes, and the water cycle</li><li>human geography, including: types of settlement and land use, economic activity including trade links, and the distribution of natural resources including energy, food, minerals and water</li></ul></li></ul>	<ul><li>use maps, atlases, globes and digital/computer mapping to locate countries and describe features studied</li><li>use the eight points of a compass, four and six-figure grid references, symbols and key (including the use of Ordnance Survey maps) to build their knowledge of the United Kingdom and the wider world</li><li>use fieldwork to observe, measure and record the human and physical features in the local area using a range of methods, including sketch maps, plans and graphs, and digital technologies</li></ul>

History	
KS1	Pupils should develop an awareness of the past, using common words and phrases relating to the passing of time. They should know where the people and events they study fit within a chronological framework and identify similarities and differences between ways of life in different periods. They should use a wide vocabulary of everyday historical terms. They should ask and answer questions, choosing and using parts of stories and other sources to show that they know and understand key features of events. They should understand some of the ways in which we find out about the past and identify different ways in which it is represented. In planning to ensure the progression described above through teaching about the people, events and changes outlined below, teachers are often introducing pupils to historical periods that they will study more fully at key stages 2 and 3. Pupils should be taught about: • changes within living memory. Where appropriate, these should be used to reveal aspects of change in national life • events beyond living memory that are significant nationally or globally (e.g. the Great Fire of London, the first aeroplane flight or events commemorated through festivals or anniversaries) • the lives of significant individuals in the past who have contributed to national and international achievements. Some should be used to compare aspects of life in different periods (e.g. Elizabeth I and Queen Victoria, Christopher Columbus and Neil Armstrong, William Caxton and Tim Berners-Lee, Pieter Bruegel the Elder and LS Lowry, Rosa Parks and Emily Davison, Mary Seacole and Edith Cavell) • significant historical events, people and places in their own locality

History	
KS2	Pupils should continue to develop a chronologically secure knowledge and understanding of British, local and world history, establishing clear narratives within and across the periods they study. They should note connections, contrasts and trends over time and develop the appropriate use of historical terms. They should regularly address and sometimes devise historically valid questions about change, cause, similarity and difference, and significance. They should construct informed responses that involve thoughtful selection and organisation of relevant historical information. They should understand how our knowledge of the past is constructed from a range of sources and that different versions of past events may exist, giving some reasons for this. In planning to ensure the progression described above through teaching the British, local and world history outlined below, teachers should combine overview and depth studies to help pupils understand both the long arc of development and the complexity of specific aspects of the content. Pupils should be taught about:

Changes in Britain from the Stone Age to the Iron Age. *This could include:*	**The Roman Empire and its impact on Britain.** *This could include:*	**Britain's settlement by Anglo-Saxons and Scots.** *This could include:*
▪ *late Neolithic hunter-gatherers and early farmers, e.g. Skara Brae* ▪ *Bronze Age religion, technology and travel, e.g. Stonehenge* ▪ *Iron Age hill forts: tribal kingdoms, farming, art and culture*	▪ *Julius Caesar's attempted invasion in 55-54 BC* ▪ *the Roman Empire by AD 42 and the power of its army* ▪ *successful invasion by Claudius and conquest, including Hadrian's Wall* ▪ *British resistance, e.g. Boudica* ▪ *"Romanisation" of Britain: sites such as Caerwent and the impact of technology, culture and beliefs, including early Christianity*	▪ *Roman withdrawal from Britain in c. AD 410 and the fall of the western Roman Empire* ▪ *Scots invasions from Ireland to north Britain (now Scotland)* ▪ *Anglo-Saxon invasions, settlements and kingdoms: place names and village life* ▪ *Anglo-Saxon art and culture* ▪ *Christian conversion – Canterbury, Iona and Lindisfarne*
The Viking and Anglo-Saxon struggle for the Kingdom of England to the time of Edward the Confessor. *This could include:*	**A local history study.** *For example:*	**A study of an aspect or theme in British history that extends pupils' chronological knowledge beyond 1066.** *For example:*
▪ *Viking raids and invasion* ▪ *resistance by Alfred the Great and Athelstan, first king of England* ▪ *further Viking invasions and Danegeld* ▪ *Anglo-Saxon laws and justice* ▪ *Edward the Confessor and his death in 1066*	▪ *a depth study linked to one of the British areas of study listed above* ▪ *a study over time tracing how several aspects national history are reflected in the locality (this can go beyond 1066)* ▪ *a study of an aspect of history or a site dating from a period beyond 1066 that is significant in the locality.*	▪ *the changing power of monarchs using case studies such as John, Anne and Victoria* ▪ *changes in an aspect of social history, such as crime and punishment from the Anglo-Saxons to the present or leisure and entertainment in the 20th Century* ▪ *the legacy of Greek or Roman culture (art, architecture or literature) on later periods in British history, including the present day* ▪ *a significant turning point in British history, e.g. the first railways or the Battle of Britain*
The achievements of the earliest civilizations – an overview of where and when the first civilizations appeared and a depth study of one of the following: Ancient Sumer; The Indus Valley; Ancient Egypt; The Shang Dynasty of Ancient China	**Ancient Greece** – a study of Greek life and achievements and their influence on the western world	**A non-European society** that provides contrasts with British history - one study chosen from: early Islamic civilization, including a study of Baghdad c. AD 900; Mayan civilization c. AD 900; Benin (West Africa) c. AD 900-1300.

Italic text is denotes non-statutory suggestions.

Languages
KS2	Teaching may be of any modern or ancient foreign language and should focus on enabling pupils to make substantial progress in one language. The teaching should provide an appropriate balance of spoken and written language and should lay the foundations for further foreign language teaching at key stage 3. It should enable pupils to understand and communicate ideas, facts and feelings in speech and writing, focused on familiar and routine matters, using their knowledge of phonology, grammatical structures and vocabulary.

The focus of study in modern languages will be on practical communication. If an ancient language is chosen the focus will be to provide a linguistic foundation for reading comprehension and an appreciation of classical civilisation. Pupils studying ancient languages may take part in simple oral exchanges, while discussion of what they read will be conducted in English. A linguistic foundation in ancient languages may support the study of modern languages at key stage 3.

Pupils should be taught to:
- listen attentively to spoken language and show understanding by joining in and responding
- explore the patterns and sounds of language through songs and rhymes and link the spelling, sound and meaning of words
- engage in conversations; ask and answer questions; express opinions and respond to those of others; seek clarification and help*
- speak in sentences, using familiar vocabulary, phrases and basic language structures
- develop accurate pronunciation and intonation so that others understand when they are reading aloud or using familiar words and phrases*
- present ideas and information orally to a range of audiences*
- read carefully and show understanding of words, phrases and simple writing
- appreciate stories, songs, poems and rhymes in the language
- broaden their vocabulary and develop their ability to understand new words that are introduced into familiar written material, including through using a dictionary
- write phrases from memory, and adapt these to create new sentences, to express ideas clearly
- describe people, places, things and actions orally* and in writing
- understand basic grammar appropriate to the language being studied, including (where relevant): feminine, masculine and neuter forms and the conjugation of high-frequency verbs; key features and patterns of the language; how to apply these, for instance, to build sentences; and how these differ from or are similar to English

The starred (*) content above will not be applicable to ancient language |

Music	
KS1	Pupils should be taught to: • use their voices expressively and creatively by singing songs and speaking chants and rhymes • play tuned and untuned instruments musically • listen with concentration and understanding to a range of high-quality live and recorded music • experiment with, create, select and combine sounds using the inter-related dimensions of music
KS2	Pupils should be taught to sing and play musically with increasing confidence and control. They should develop an understanding of musical composition, organising and manipulating ideas within musical structures and reproducing sounds from aural memory. Pupils should be taught to: • play and perform in solo and ensemble contexts, using their voices and playing musical instruments with increasing accuracy, fluency, control and expression • improvise and compose music for a range of purposes using the inter-related dimensions of music • listen with attention to detail and recall sounds with increasing aural memory • use and understand staff and other musical notations • appreciate and understand a wide range of high-quality live and recorded music drawn from different traditions and from great composers and musicians • develop an understanding of the history of music

Physical education	
KS1	Pupils should develop fundamental movement skills, become increasingly competent and confident and access a broad range of opportunities to extend their agility, balance and coordination, individually and with others. They should be able to engage in competitive (both against self and against others) and co-operative physical activities, in a range of increasingly challenging situations. Pupils should be taught to: • master basic movements including running, jumping, throwing and catching, as well as developing balance, agility and co-ordination, and begin to apply these in a range of activities • participate in team games, developing simple tactics for attacking and defending • perform dances using simple movement patterns
KS2	Pupils should continue to apply and develop a broader range of skills, learning how to use them in different ways and to link them to make actions and sequences of movement. They should enjoy communicating, collaborating and competing with each other. They should develop an understanding of how to improve in different physical activities and sports and learn how to evaluate and recognise their own success. Pupils should be taught to: • use running, jumping, throwing and catching in isolation and in combination • play competitive games, modified where appropriate, e.g. badminton, basketball, cricket, football, hockey, netball, rounders and tennis, and apply basic principles suitable for attacking and defending • develop flexibility, strength, technique, control and balance, e.g. through athletics and gymnastics • perform dances using a range of movement patterns • take part in outdoor and adventurous activity challenges both individually and within a team • compare their performances with previous ones and demonstrate improvement to achieve their personal best
Swim	Swimming and water safety All schools must provide swimming instruction either in key stage 1 or key stage 2. In particular, pupils should be taught to: • swim competently, confidently and proficiently over a distance of at least 25 metres • use a range of strokes effectively such as front crawl, backstroke and breaststroke • perform safe self-rescue in different water-based situations.